SENSATIONAL

ALISON HOLST & SIMON HOLST

First published in 1999 by
Hyndman Publishing
PO Box 5017, Dunedin

ISBN 1-877168-33-5

TEXT
© Simon & Alison Holst

DESIGNER
Rob Di Leva

PHOTOGRAPHY
Lindsay Keats, Cover & pages
1, 4, 17, 21, 28, 33, 37, 41,
45, 49, 53, & 56
Sal Criscillo, pages 8, 12, 13,
& 25

HOME ECONOMISTS
Simon & Alison Holst

PRINTING
Tablet Colour Print
1st Reprint December 1999

Because ovens and microwave ovens
vary so much, you should take the
cooking times suggested in recipes as
guides only. The first time you make a
recipe, check it at intervals to make
sure it is not cooking faster, or more
slowly than expected.

Always follow the detailed instructions
given by manufacturers of your
appliances and equipment, rather then
the more general instructions given in
these recipes.

Acknowledgements

We would like to thank the firms who provided us with the
following food and products.

ALISON'S CHOICE Dried fruit, nuts, seeds, etc.

BENNICK'S POULTRY FARM, BULLER RD, LEVIN Fresh eggs

EMPIRE FOODSTUFFS Dried herbs and spices

FERNDALE Parmesan cheese

GENOESE FOODS Pesto

UNIFOODS John West seasonings

LUPI Olive oil and Balsamic vinegar

SUREBRAND Teflon liners

TARARUA Grated cheese and cultured dairy products

SALAD VEGETABLES If you are a keen and adventurous
gardener and want to grow interesting and unusual salad
vegetables and herbs, contact Kings Seeds (NZ) Ltd, who
have an excellent mail order seed catalogue, PO Box 283,
Katikati, Phone: (07) 549 3409, Fax: (07) 549 3408.

Important Information

For best results, use a standard metric (250ml) measuring
cup and metric measuring spoons when you use these
recipes. We use the following standards: 1 tablespoon holds
15ml and 1 teaspoon holds 5ml.

All the cup and spoon measures in the recipes are level,
unless otherwise stated. Sets of measuring cups make it
easier to measure ¼ and ½ cup quantities.

ABBREVIATIONS USED:

cm	centimetre	ml	millilitre
tsp	teaspoon	°C	Celsius
g	gram	Tbsp	tablespoon

We used a 720 Watt microwave oven to cook the
microwaved foods in this book. Microwave cooking times are
given as a guide only. Alter times to suit the wattage of the
microwave oven you use.

COVER PHOTO: East-West Beef Salad with Coriander Dressing, page 48
TITLE PAGE PHOTO: Chicken & Crispy Noodle Salad, page 54

Contents

About This Book

A good flavourful salad with just enough interesting dressing to liven it up is a real treat! When we asked members of the audience at cooking demonstrations to tell us what topics they would like us to write about – top of their list was salads! Many people added a note to say that they loved the interesting salads they were given when they ate out, but they felt that those they made themselves were boring!

We hope that this book will help you to produce side salads that are popular, lively and just a little different. Why not try serving interesting and substantial salads as the main part of your meal, especially in warmer weather? We have found that such salads can delight people who we thought would have preferred something more conventional.

We are lucky to have a wonderful range of inviting salad ingredients readily available in all seasons, and also to have at our fingertips the makings of dressings that will really add zest to our salads! With good nutrition in mind, we suggest that you enjoy generous quantities of healthful vegetables in your salads, and add just enough flavourful dressing to coat these very lightly.

Remember too, that variety is the spice of life. Do try a wide range of our salads.

We hope you enjoy them as much as we do!

Simon and Alison Holst

OPPOSITE: Californian Pasta Salad, page 34

Healthy Eating

We all want to live long and healthy lives! But how? Eating more salads (or fruit and vegetables in general) may be a good start.

We've all heard it said that "good clean living" and maintaining a "healthy (or rather healthful) diet" are keys to this goal. These sayings appear to be borne out – more and more scientific research is emphasising the importance of eating well.

This is not necessarily surprising as, after all, we are quite literally what we eat! Better still, you don't even have to stop eating everything you like – it is moderation that matters! Small, easy to make changes may result in appreciable health benefits. This is great news to those like us, who believe that "We don't live to be healthy – we live better by being healthy!" With a sensible, varied and balanced diet coupled with regular, moderate exercise we are taking an important step towards good health and well being.

Although there are many different ideas about good nutrition, there is one area of general consensus – we should all try to include plenty of vegetables and fruit in our diet everyday. By now we're sure that you are all familiar with the "5 plus a day" message that encourages eating at least five servings of vegetables and fruit per day.

There are many reasons why fruit and vegetables are so good for us. Not only do they add interesting flavours and variety to our diets, they are full of vitamins and minerals (including important antioxidants), are high in complex carbohydrates and fibre, low in salt, and (generally) low in fat. (While vitamins and minerals can also be supplied in the form of pills or supplements, there is growing evidence that these do not provide the same health benefits as those obtained from natural foods.)

Obviously, eating plenty of salads is an excellent way to increase your vegetable (and even fruit) intake. Serving a side salad with your meal (either as a side dish or as a salad course) is one way to eat more vegetables, but why not consider going one step further and making a salad the focus or main part of your meal.

We have divided this book into two roughly evenly sized sections, Simple & Side Salads and Main Dish Salads. Both include a range of interesting salads that can be made either using seasonal produce, or ingredients that are available year round – this means that you can enjoy salads with or as your meal year round, regardless of the season.

Eating more salads is an important step in the right direction. For an overall picture of dietary recommendations, check out the information below (based on the New Zealand Nutrition Guidelines, 1995).

What Should We Eat?

1. Eat a variety of foods from these major food groups every day:

Vegetables and fruits – high in vitamins (including antioxidants) and minerals, and a good source of fibre. Aim for at least 5 servings per day (3 vegetable, 2 fruit).

Breads and cereal foods – high in complex carbohydrates and fibre (especially whole grain products). Aim for at least 6 servings per day.

Milk and milk products – good source of protein and some vitamins and minerals, especially calcium. Aim for at least 2 servings per day, preferably low fat.

Lean meats, chicken, fish, eggs, nuts or pulses – good sources of protein and some vitamins and minerals, especially iron (particularly lean red meat). Aim for at least 1 serving of any one of these per day.

2. Prepare meals with minimal added fat (especially saturated fat) and salt.

All fat is rich in energy (9 kilocalories per gram), so excessive intake should be avoided, especially if you are trying to lose weight.

Fat can broadly be divided into two categories: **unsaturated** fats (including both **mono-** and **poly-** unsaturated); and **saturated** fats including **trans**-fats which have a similar effect.

Saturated and trans fats raise blood cholesterol. Fatty meat and full-cream dairy products are high in saturated fats, as are coconut and palm oil. Trans-fats are found in some meat and dairy products, but also some processed vegetable fats like some margarines (less than 1%) and commercial frying fats.

Mono- and polyunsaturated fats actually tend to lower blood cholesterol (although they do so in different ways). Vegetable oils such as grapeseed, corn and safflower are rich in polyunsaturated fats. Olive and canola oil are particularly good sources of monounsaturated fats (which is why we have used them in this book, in preference to other vegetable oils).

Nuts (although high in energy) and seeds are a good source of mono- and polyunsaturated fats, including Omega-3 fatty acids which may be protective against heart disease (as well as a good source of other vitamins and minerals). Some studies have indicated that eating a handful of nuts (30g) a day may help protect against heart (and other disease). They make a delicious and nutritious addition to almost any salad, so why not keep plenty on hand and add a handful here and there.

Remember, most foods contain mixtures of monounsaturated fats, polyunsaturated fats and saturated fats – this means that reducing total fat consumption also tends to reduce saturated fat intake.

Add salt sparingly when cooking – why not try replacing it with other flavourful and interesting ingredients such as herbs and spices.

3. Choose pre-prepared foods, drinks and snacks that are low in fat (especially saturated fats), salt and sugar.

It is easy to control the amounts of fat, salt and sugar in foods we cook at home, but foods prepared outside the home, like meals at restaurants, takeaways and even convenience foods from the supermarket (frozen meals, pizzas etc.) can be sources of 'hidden' fat, sugar and salt. Ask for advice on low fat options and/or read the nutritional information on labels when making your selection.

This is particularly true for salt (which can contribute to hypertension). Up to three quarters of the salt we eat comes from processed foods. While we should use salt sparingly when cooking, it is far more important to be aware of the amount that may be contained in processed foods. Fresh foods such as vegetables are naturally low in salt so are a good option, or look for low-salt (low-sodium) or reduced-salt labels on processed foods.

4. Maintain a healthy body weight by regular physical activity and healthy eating.

The energy you consume (what you eat) should be balanced with the energy you use (everything you do uses energy, but the more vigorous the activity, the more energy you use). If you are getting more energy than you need from the food you eat (be it from fat, alcohol, protein or carbohydrate), your body will tend to store it as fat.

If you want to lose weight, you should try to decrease the amount of energy you are eating and increase the amount of exercise you are doing. (Remember small, gradual changes are often the most effective.)

The body mass index (BMI) can be used to determine if your weight is in the "healthy" range. To calculate your BMI, divide your weight (in kilograms) by your height (in metres) squared ie

$$BMI = \frac{weight\ in\ (kg)}{height\ in\ (m)^2}$$

The healthy range is usually somewhere between 20–25, but depends on age and sex. (Talk to your doctor or other health professional for more details.)

5. Drink plenty of liquids everyday.

Your body loses 1–1.5 litres of water a day, so it needs to be replaced by at least this amount. Some water is obtained from the food we eat, but we should still aim to drink 1-2 litres of water (or other drinks like tea or coffee) per day. You should drink more if it is hot or you are exercising.

6. If drinking alcohol, do so in moderation.

There has been much well publicised debate about the health benefits (or detriments) associated with drinking alcohol. While it now appears that there may be some benefit (or little harm) from a drink or two per day (especially of wine), alcohol should be consumed in moderation. Women should drink no more than 20g of alcohol per day (1–2 glasses of wine), and men no more than 30g per day (2–3 glasses of wine).

Remember, too, that alcohol is high in energy (containing 7 kilocalories per gram. It is more energy dense than protein or carbohydrate).

Simple & Side Salads

Salads are so versatile!

They are a great way to serve vegetables and these interesting salads will add colour, crunch and a dash of flavour to a main course. Or for something different, try serving them as a starter course on their own.

We have included a wide selection of our favourite starters or side salads, with suggestions on how to serve them, so that you will be able to find a suitable salad whatever the season.

Don't hesitate to mix and match our salad ingredients with different dressings to make your own creations.

OPPOSITE: Mixed Green Salad, page 10

simple salads and dressings

- raw apple cubes (tossed in dressing to stop browning)
- avocado halves, slices or cubes
- lightly cooked asparagus spears
- lightly cooked green beans, chopped
- beansprouts, pea sprouts, sunflower sprouts, etc
- beetroot, especially baby, canned
- shredded cabbage
- shredded raw carrots or sliced cooked carrots
- cauliflower florets, raw or lightly cooked
- thinly sliced or lightly cooked sliced celery
- coleslaw mixes (undressed)
- corn kernels, roasted, boiled, canned or frozen
- thinly sliced daikon (Japanese radish)
- kiwifruit slices or cubes
- cooked sliced kumara
- lettuce, in chunky pieces, torn or sliced
- mesclun (baby salad leaves)
- button mushrooms, sliced
- peas, cooked
- raw sugarpeas in their pods, or snowpeas
- raw pears, sliced (tossed in dressing to stop browning)
- peppers, raw or roasted, all colours
- cooked waxy potatoes
- radishes
- small or torn spinach leaves
- swede, raw, shredded,
- raw small or large tomatoes
- watercress sprigs or leaves
- zucchini, lightly cooked or raw

Salads don't have to be complicated – in fact simple salads are sometimes better than those which contain many ingredients.

Here are some suggestions of suitable salad 'base' ingredients, but we are sure you can think of more.

Our fastest salads are made of one vegetable, a tub of mesclun (mixed baby salad leaves) or a bag of sprouts or undressed coleslaw from the supermarket, tossed in a made-ahead dressing from the refrigerator.

Try any of the easy dressings on the following page, drizzling them over single vegetables, then try mixtures of two, three or even more of the vegetables listed here. (You need not limit yourself to raw vegetables either — why not try warm or cold cooked vegetables, or even raw fruit.)

If you have leftovers and want a salad for lunch, just add cooked rice or pasta, toasted bread cubes or well-drained canned beans, cooked chicken or canned fish to some of these vegetables, and drizzle with one of our easy dressings.

For really quick **"dressing-less" salads**, sprinkle the prepared vegetable(s) with lemon juice and sprinkle lightly with bought "spicy herb seasoning salt" or other mixtures of dried herbs, spices and salt.

french dressing

This is a good basic all-purpose dressing, which you can put together in a few minutes and keep in your refrigerator. The mustard in it is important, since it stops the dressing separating.

¼ cup olive or canola oil
2 tsp wine vinegar
1 tsp Dijon or mild mustard
¼ tsp salt
1 tsp sugar

Combine all ingredients in a screw-topped jar and shake. Refrigerate up to a week. Shake again before use.

Add to raw or cooked vegetables and raw fruit just before serving.

italian dressing

Combine the ingredients for French dressing plus 1 teaspoon of tomato paste together in a screw-topped jar. Taste to see whether the dressing has a definite tomato flavour. If not, add another teaspoon of tomato paste and shake again. Add a tablespoon of water if the dressing becomes too thick. Refrigerate up to a week.

herbed dressing

Shake the ingredients for French Dressing with 1–2 tablespoons very finely chopped fresh herbs (suitable herbs include parsley, chives, dill, tarragon, thyme, and rosemary). Use one or more herbs, depending on your taste and what is available. Replace the salt with ¼ teaspoon of herb salt or garlic, onion or celery salt if desired.

extra-lite dressing

If you want a salad dressing which is virtually fat-free, try the following recipe and its variations.

1 Tbsp cornflour
½ tsp garlic salt
½ tsp celery salt
1 tsp sugar
1 cup cold water
1 Tbsp Dijon or mild mustard
1 Tbsp lemon juice
1 Tbsp wine vinegar
2 Tbsp chopped fresh herbs
   (optional)

Mix the first five ingredients in a small pot and bring to the boil, stirring all the time, till mixture is smooth and thick. Remove from heat and whisk in the remaining ingredients. Refrigerate and use within a week.

For Italian Extra-Lite Dressing, add 2 tsp tomato paste.

For a Creamy Extra-Lite Dressing, mix equal parts of dressing and low-fat natural yoghurt, and add chopped fresh or dried dill leaves, if available.

caesar salad

Caesar salad is justifiably popular as a starter, side salad, or main. Always make it with Cos lettuce.

FOR 4–6 SERVINGS:
1 Cos (Romaine) lettuce
¼–½ cup freshly grated
    Parmesan cheese
½–1 cup croutons (see page 60)

DRESSING:
1 egg
1 clove garlic
juice of 1 lime or lemon
2 anchovy fillets
1 tsp Dijon or mild mustard
about ½ tsp salt
freshly ground black pepper
¼–½ cup olive oil

Wash lettuce leaves. Roll up damp leaves in a length of paper towels to dry well. Chill for several hours, or overnight, so leaves are dry and cold when used.

Combine all dressing ingredients except oil in a food processor or blender. Blend until smooth, then, with motor running, add oil in a slow steady stream until the dressing is as thick as pouring cream. Season to taste.

To assemble the salad, arrange leaves in a large salad bowl, sprinkling croutons through them. Just before serving, drizzle dressing over leaves, toss if desired, then sprinkle with Parmesan.

VARIATIONS: For a lighter dressing, leave out the egg. For Chicken Caesar Salad, serve larger salad portions, and add 50–100g of cooked chicken per serving.

spinach salad

This popular salad may be served as a side salad, or in larger amounts as a full meal.

FOR 4-6 SERVINGS:
400–500g good quality small
    spinach leaves
4–6 rashers lean bacon
250g button mushrooms
a few canned water chestnuts
    (optional)
avocado (optional)
½–1 cup small croutons (see
    page 60)

DRESSING:
¼ cup canola or olive oil
¼ tsp salt, approximately
1 tsp sugar
2–3 tsp Dijon or mild mustard
2 Tbsp wine vinegar

Wash the spinach carefully in a sink of cold water. Handle carefully to avoid bruising. Roll in a clean teatowel or length of paper towels and refrigerate, making sure that the leaves are dry before using them in the salad.

Remove rinds and grill bacon until crisp. Chop or break bacon into small pieces and set aside.

Make the dressing by mixing all ingredients in a screw-topped jar. Leave at room temperature until required.

Just before serving, wash, dry and slice the mushrooms, drain and slice canned water chestnuts and slice avocado if using. Put with the cold dry spinach and the bacon in a large serving bowl or plastic bag, then pour the dressing over them and toss gently until the spinach is coated. Arrange in individual bowls and sprinkle generously with croutons. Serve promptly.

memorable coleslaws

Coleslaw is an amazingly useful and versatile salad which doesn't call for anything exotic or expensive! Its ingredients will keep in the refrigerator for days and are readily available right through the year. It is one of the few leafy salads which may be made ahead, so is suitable for pot-luck meals and picnics. Picky young eaters often like coleslaw because they know what it is. As well, coleslaw need never be boring, because you can make so many variations.

For basic coleslaw, simply shred quarter of a drum-head cabbage very finely (with a sharp knife or a food-processor slicing blade), coarsely grate a scrubbed carrot or two (with a hand grater or the shredding blade of a food processor), and toss the two together with any of the dressings on pages 58 to 61. (Our favourite coleslaw dressing is Sesame Dressing, page 60.)

- Other suitable vegetable additions are thinly sliced celery, peppers, cauliflower and spring onions. Bean sprouts and pea sprouts give coleslaw a lovely, slightly nutty flavour.

- For sweetness add small cubes of unpeeled apple tossed in lemon juice, sultanas, currants or Californian raisins.

- Grated cheese is a popular addition to basic cabbage, carrot and celery coleslaw.

- Add toasted seeds and nuts (page 60) for a change.

Two Minute Noodle Coleslaw

Partially break up the noodles from a packet of Two Minute Noodles. Place on foil and heat under a moderate grill until noodles turn golden brown (1–2 minutes). Break into smaller pieces, and toss through coleslaw which has been tossed with Sesame Dressing (page 60), just moments before it is to be eaten. Note: Don't do this too often since these noodles are usually fried in palm oil (a saturated plant oil) before you get them.

Easy Oriental Coleslaw

Using quantities to suit, shred cabbage and celery and grate carrot, by hand or in a food processor. Add beansprouts if you have them, and a few chopped roasted peanuts, and add just enough Sesame Dressing (page 60) to moisten everything. Serve immediately.

carrot and apple salad

These flavours complement each other to make a good winter salad.

FOR 2 SERVINGS:
1 carrot, grated
2 tart (preferably Sturmer)
  apples
2–4 Tbsp sultanas or currants
salad greens (optional)

DRESSING:
2–3 Tbsp mayonnaise (page 58)
1–2 Tbsp orange juice

Measure the mayonnaise into a small bowl and then mix to consistency of thick cream with orange juice.

Grate the carrot and unpeeled apples into long shreds. Add sultanas and enough thinned mayonnaise to coat the carrot and apple.

Serve in a bowl, by itself, or on salad greens, plain or sprinkled with chopped walnuts, roasted sunflower seeds or toasted sesame seeds.

spicy carrot salad

This salad is as good with curries as it is with barbecues.

FOR 4 SERVINGS:
2 large carrots
1 spring onion, finely chopped
2–4 Tbsp finely chopped mint
  or coriander leaves
1 tsp finely grated root ginger
2 Tbsp lemon juice

Shred the carrots coarsely. Toss with the finely chopped spring onion, the chopped mint or coriander leaves, ginger and lemon juice. Use immediately, or refrigerate in a plastic bag, up to 2 days.

VARIATIONS: For a Sweet & Sour salad, add 1 tablespoon each of honey and Dijon mustard to the mixture. For a more substantial salad, try adding ½–1 cup chopped roasted peanuts too.

cooked carrot salad

Cooked carrots, in a well flavoured tomato dressing, make a good addition to a salad table.

FOR 4 SERVINGS:
400–500g carrots

DRESSING:
½ packet tomato soup
½ cup water
¼ cup wine vinegar
3 Tbsp olive or canola oil
2–3 Tbsp sugar

Scrub or thinly peel carrots and slice crossways, 5mm thick. Cover and cook without seasonings in a small amount of water until barely tender. (Add some leeks, green pepper or celery two minutes before the carrots are cooked, for contrasting colours, textures and flavours, if you like.) Drain off any remaining water.

While carrots cook, simmer soup and water for 3 minutes. Add vinegar, oil and half the sugar and simmer 2 minutes longer. Taste and add extra sugar, if necessary. Pour half this dressing over the hot drained vegetables. Cover and leave in the dressing to cool.

Stir just before serving, adding extra dressing and fresh herbs to garnish if desired.

bird's nest salad (See picture opposite)

This salad is a talking point – different, interesting, and very popular. Rice vermicelli noodles keep "for ever" in your store cupboard. Cook them at the last minute, letting your family or friends watch the exciting procedure.

FOR 4-6 SERVINGS:
about 50g dry rice vermicelli
  noodles
oil for frying
about 4 cups salad greens*
¼ cup chopped coriander
  leaves
½ cup roughly chopped
  roasted peanuts

DRESSING:
1 clove garlic, very finely
  chopped
½ tsp chilli paste
1 Tbsp each sugar and sesame
  oil
1 Tbsp rice vinegar or wine
  vinegar
2 Tbsp each water and fish
  sauce

* mesclun, lettuce,
  beansprouts, chopped spring
  onions, etc.

Make the dressing by shaking all the dressing ingredients together in an airtight jar.

Pull the rice noodles away from the block and cut into shorter lengths for easier handling, if you like. Heat oil about 1cm deep in a wok or medium-sized pot or pan until one or two noodles dropped in it puff up. Keeping oil at this heat, fry noodles in small handfuls, turning them with tongs when the under-side is puffed. They should be very lightly coloured (but not brown) rather than white. Drain and cool on paper towels. (Make ahead and store up to an hour in an airtight plastic bag if you like.)

Assemble salad 30 seconds before serving. Toss together the noodles, salad greens, other salad additions, chopped coriander and most of the peanuts (always use very fresh peanuts). Add half the dressing, toss, then taste, adding more if desired.

spinach and apple salad

Although the combination may seem unusual, this salad is crunchy and refreshing.

FOR 4-6 SERVINGS:
4 cups good quality spinach
  leaves
½ mild onion, in rings
1 apple, in thin wedges
1–2 Tbsp sultanas, chopped

DRESSING:
2 Tbsp wine vinegar
2 Tbsp canola or olive oil
1 tsp Dijon or mild mustard
½ tsp sugar
¼ tsp salt

Prepare spinach as in recipe on page 13. In a wide salad bowl, combine the dressing ingredients, then add the onion rings, thin wedges of unpeeled apple and chopped sultanas. Toss gently.

Just before serving, tear the cold dry spinach into bite-sized pieces, add to the bowl and toss the apple and dressing mixture through the spinach.

celery and apple salad

This popular winter salad is quickly made and has an interesting texture.

FOR 2-4 SERVINGS:
2 stalks celery
2 apples
2–3 Tbsp mayonnaise (page 58)
2 Tbsp chopped walnuts

Cut the celery and unpeeled apple into 5mm cubes. Thin the mayonnaise to pouring consistency with warm water, mix it with the celery and apple, then sprinkle with chopped walnuts.

mushroom salad

Even people who think they do not like raw mushrooms will usually enjoy this salad with its delicious herby, mustardy dressing. Firm fresh mushrooms are essential.

FOR 4-6 SERVINGS:
200–300g clean button mushrooms

DRESSING:
2 Tbsp white wine vinegar or
   lemon juice
¼ cup canola oil
½ tsp each salt, sugar and
   freshly ground black pepper
2–3 tsp Dijon or mild mustard
2 Tbsp finely chopped parsley

Shake together or food process dressing ingredients. Just before serving, slice the mushrooms and toss with enough dressing to coat them.

marinated leek salad

Lightly cooked leeks make a very interesting winter salad.

FOR 2–3 SERVINGS:
2 leeks, sliced
3–4 Tbsp chopped roasted
   cashew nuts

DRESSING:
¼ cup olive or canola oil
2 Tbsp wine vinegar
1 clove garlic, crushed
2 tsp Dijon or mild mustard
salt and pepper to taste

Peel tough outer leaves off leek(s) and wash well under running water. Cut into slices about 7mm thick, using all the white but only the tender inner layers of the green portion. Cook in a little water until just soft, but still tender and bright green. Refresh with cold water and drain well, then spread out on paper towels to dry completely.

Shake all dressing ingredients in a screw-topped jar. Pour dressing over cooled leeks and leave for at least 1 hour before serving at room temperature, sprinkled with nuts.

"brocauli" salad

A salad made from a mixture of lightly cooked broccoli and cauliflower may be made at most times of the year. Eat it as soon as you coat the cooked vegetables with dressing, or make it up to 24 hours ahead.

FOR 4 SERVINGS:
200–250g prepared broccoli
250–300g prepared cauliflower

DRESSING:
¼ cup olive or canola oil
3 Tbsp white wine vinegar
1 clove garlic, finely chopped
½ tsp dried oreganum,
   crumbled
1–2 tsp Dijon or mild mustard
salt and pepper to taste

Cut vegetables into bite-sized pieces, peeling off and discarding any tough outer skin, then boil in a little lightly salted water, until tender-crisp. Cool to room temperature in very cold water, then drain and refrigerate in a plastic bag if not using immediately.

Measure dressing ingredients except salt and pepper, into a screw-topped jar and shake well. Season to taste.

To keep broccoli bright green, toss the vegetables in the dressing just before serving. For more flavour, but olive-coloured broccoli, mix the dressing and vegetables as soon as both are prepared and leave to stand.

kumara salad

Kumara make very satisfying salads. Leave out some of the additions if you want to. The dressing is good with and without the sour cream (or yoghurt).

ABOUT 6 SERVINGS:
3 orange-fleshed kumara
   (750g)
¼ cup sultanas
1 firm banana
¼–½ cup shredded coconut
   (optional)
2 spring onions, finely
   chopped
roasted peanuts or cashews
   (optional)

DRESSING:
¼ cup olive or canola oil
¼ cup white wine vinegar
1 tsp Dijon or mild mustard
1–2 tsp grated root ginger
½ tsp salt
2 tsp sugar
¼ cup lite sour cream or plain
   low fat yoghurt (optional)

Shake first six dressing ingredients in a screw-topped jar. Add sour cream or yoghurt for a creamy dressing.

Microwave the scrubbed kumara until tender. When cool enough to handle, peel and chop in bite-sized pieces.

Pour boiling water over sultanas to plump them up, then drain well and mix through the kumara. Add sliced banana, coconut (if using) and spring onions.

Toss with half the dressing, adding more when serving, if desired. Sprinkle with chopped nuts.

warm stuffed peppers

Made when peppers are at their best, these look and taste spectacular!

FOR 4–8 SERVINGS:
4 red or yellow peppers
8 basil leaves
2 cloves garlic, thinly sliced
8 anchovy fillets
about 16 capers
6 medium tomatoes, or
    canned whole tomatoes
8–16 black olives
about ¼ cup olive oil
fresh basil leaves for garnish

Halve peppers lengthways, remove pith and seeds, then place in one layer in a shallow, foil-lined roasting dish.

Place a basil leaf, several slices of garlic, an anchovy fillet and two capers in each pepper half.

Quarter or halve tomatoes, removing seeds and liquid. Place pieces, cut sides down, in peppers, top with olives and drizzle 1–2 teaspoons of olive oil over each.

Bake uncovered, at 200°C for about 45 minutes, until edges are lightly charred. Serve warm or at room temperature, garnished with basil leaves, with chunks of bread to mop up juices.

avocado with mediterranean dressing

Serve these halved avocados as an impressive starter!

FOR 4 SERVINGS:
2 medium sized ripe avocados

DRESSING:
2 Tbsp olive oil
¼ cup pinenuts
4 sundried tomatoes, chopped
2 tsp Balsamic or wine
    vinegar
1 clove garlic, very finely
    chopped
salt and pepper to taste

Warm a little of the olive oil in a frypan, add the pinenuts and heat until golden brown. Add the rest of the oil and remaining dressing ingredients, season to taste and set aside until required (can be prepared up to 24 hours in advance).

Just before serving, halve the avocados and remove the stone. Spoon the dressing into the cavities and serve!

spiced tomato (and cucumber) salad

Really simple salads never go out of fashion. Serve it at picnics and barbecues, or with curries.

FOR 4–6 SERVINGS:
3–4 red, firm, flavourful tomatoes
½ telegraph cucumber (optional)
2 spring onions or ¼ red onion
1 Tbsp sugar
1–2 tsp ground cumin
½ tsp salt
chopped coriander (optional)

Cut tomatoes in neat 1cm cubes. If using, cut unpeeled cucumber into similar cubes. Slice spring onions thinly or finely chop the red onion. Place prepared vegetables in a serving dish. A few minutes before serving, sprinkle with the sugar, cumin and salt, then mix gently. (Use smaller amount of cumin if not using cucumber.) Sprinkle with coriander leaves, if available, and serve cold.

tomato & mozzarella salad

This colourful salad is an Italian classic and is as good served as a starter as it is as part of a buffet, with barbecues, or for vegetarians.

FOR 4–6 SERVINGS:
4–6 ripe tomatoes
125–250g Mozzarella cheese*
salt and pepper to taste
2 Tbsp olive oil
chopped fresh basil to garnish

Cut the tomatoes in slices 1cm thick and slice Mozzarella thinly. Arrange alternate slices of tomato and cheese on a flat plate, so slices overlap. Sprinkle with salt and pepper to taste, then drizzle olive oil over the salad. Top with chopped fresh basil just before serving.

*Look for roundish balls of Mozzarella.

marinated tomato salad

It's hard to beat this salad, made from ripe, red tomatoes from your own garden!

FOR 4 SERVINGS:
5–6 tomatoes
1 tsp sugar
¼–½ tsp salt
black pepper to taste
few drops Tabasco sauce
2–3 tsp wine vinegar
1 Tbsp chopped basil
1–2 Tbsp olive or canola oil
(optional)

Slice, quarter or cube the tomatoes into a serving dish.

About 10–15 minutes before serving, sprinkle the remaining ingredients, in the order given, over the tomatoes. Toss lightly and leave to stand at room temperature.

NOTE: Replace basil with fresh coriander leaves or parsley.

elizabeth's favourite salad

Alison's granddaughters Elizabeth and Jennifer, will make (and eat!) this ever-popular salad very willingly, at the drop of a hat!

FOR 4 SERVINGS:
1 Tbsp lemon juice
1 tsp sugar
¼ tsp salt
1 large avocado
2–3 firm, red tomatoes
10cm length telegraph
    cucumber
about 2 cups of chopped
    crisp-leaf lettuce
1–2 spring onions
1 Tbsp olive or canola oil
freshly ground pepper to taste

A short time before serving, mix the lemon juice, sugar and salt in the bottom of a fairly large salad bowl. Cut the stoned, peeled avocado into 1cm cubes and turn gently in the lemon juice. Add the tomatoes and unpeeled cucumber, cut in similar cubes.

Cut part of a firm hearty (iceberg) lettuce into 1–2cm squares and add with the chopped spring onions to salad bowl.

Sprinkle with oil and pepper, and toss gently to mix everything.

wilted cucumber salad

A good side dish for a curry, or grilled lamb with a peanutty sauce.

FOR 4-6 SERVINGS:
1 telegraph cucumber
1 tsp salt in 1 cup water
2 spring onions, chopped
1 small clove garlic, finely
    chopped (optional)
2 Tbsp wine vinegar
pinch chilli powder
1 Tbsp each toasted sesame
    seeds and sugar

Halve cucumber lengthways. Scoop out the seeds using a teaspoon. Cut in thin slices and stand these in the salted water, for 10 minutes or longer.

When serving, drain cucumber well. Place in serving dish with spring onion, garlic, vinegar and chilli powder. Crush toasted sesame seeds with the sugar in a pestle and mortar (or blender), add to the salad and mix well.

mexican salad

A colourful salad that is best made ahead.

FOR 6-8 SERVINGS:
2 large tomatoes
1–2 sticks celery
1 red and 1 green pepper
1 cup each corn kernels,
    cucumber cubes and
    chopped cooked green
    beans
2–4 Tbsp chopped coriander

DRESSING:
¼ cup olive or canola oil
2 Tbsp sugar
finely grated rind of 1 lime or
    ½ lemon
¼ cup lime or lemon juice
2 cloves garlic, finely chopped
½ tsp each ground cumin and
    salt
about ¼ tsp chilli powder

Cut all vegetables into small pieces about the same size as the corn and mix in a bowl. Shake the dressing ingredients together in a jar, then add to the vegetables.

Mix the dressing gently but thoroughly through the vegetables, then leave to stand in the refrigerator for at least 15 minutes or up to 2 hours.

Toss coriander through salad just before serving.

asparagus salad

To us, asparagus means spring! Make this salad the star attraction of your meal.

FOR 4 SERVINGS:
16–20 spears of asparagus
1 Tbsp finely chopped parsley
    or chives
1 hardboiled egg, chopped or
    ½ red pepper, sliced

DRESSING:
1 Tbsp wine vinegar
1 Tbsp lemon juice
½ tsp salt
1 tsp Dijon or mild mustard
2–3 Tbsp olive or canola oil
2 Tbsp lite sour cream
    (optional)

Snap tough bases from asparagus stalks and microwave, grill or stir-fry-steam, until tender crisp and still bright green. Place on a serving dish, with all tips in the same direction. Cover and refrigerate until serving.

Shake all dressing ingredients in a screw-topped jar. Just before serving, pour dressing evenly over the asparagus and sprinkle the chopped egg or red pepper strips in a band across the central part of the stems.

NOTE: For a simpler dressing, drizzle a little lemon juice and olive oil over the asparagus.

roasted vegetable salads (See picture opposite)

Vegetables cooked this way develop an excellent flavour and an interesting texture, and may be served warm or at room temperature, as interesting salads, singly or in mixtures. Use vegetables such as peppers (capsicums), zucchini, thick asparagus stalks, large mushrooms, eggplant, red onions, young beetroot, etc., and cook until their flesh is tender and the edges are charred.

Cut your chosen vegetables into chunky pieces, removing pith and seeds from peppers and stems from mushrooms. Quarter onions so pieces are held together by the root.

Brush lightly with olive oil or Seasoned Oil (page 61). Cook in a double-sided contact grill preheated to medium, for about 5 minutes, or under a regular grill, turning after half time, for 10-15 minutes, or roast uncovered at 200°C for 20–30 minutes, removing mushrooms before other vegetables if necessary. (Exact times depend on the size and thickness of the vegetable pieces.)

Remove skins from peppers if desired. Serve roasted vegetables warm or at room temperature, exactly as they are, or drizzled with a little extra plain or seasoned oil, and a squeeze of lemon juice or a few drops of Balsamic vinegar, OR drizzle with Roasted Vegetable Salad Dressing (page 61) or with Poppy Seed Dressing (page 61).

Serve salad garnished with black olives and sprigs of suitable fresh herbs, if desired.

roasted red onion salad (See picture opposite)

Red onions are milder than other onions, and make an interesting and different salad.

FOR 4 SERVINGS:
4 red onions, quartered and
     roasted*
1 Tbsp olive oil
2 tsp wine vinegar
1 tsp Balsamic vinegar
1 tsp sugar
½ tsp finely chopped fresh
     sage or thyme (optional)

Roast the quartered red onions without removing their roots (*as for Roasted Vegetable Salads). While they cook, mix the remaining ingredients in a screw-topped jar to make a dressing.

While hot (or warm) transfer the roasted onions to a serving dish, sprinkle with dressing and turn lightly to coat, without breaking up the onions.

Serve warm or at room temperature (but not chilled) with barbecued foods.

VARIATION: Brush with Seasoned Oil (page 61) instead of olive oil.

warm green bean salad

This delicious, simple salad is especially good with small tender green beans.

FOR 4–6 SERVINGS:
500g young tender green
   beans
1 cup finely chopped celery

DRESSING:
2 garlic cloves, finely chopped
2–3 Tbsp olive or canola oil
2 Tbsp wine vinegar
1 tsp Dijon or mild mustard
½ tsp each salt and sugar

Leave small beans whole and cut larger beans into thick slices. Boil briskly until tender-crisp, then drain.

While beans cook, make the dressing. Heat chopped garlic in oil. Remove from heat and add the remaining dressing ingredients.

Tip dressing and chopped celery on to the hot drained beans. For best flavour, leave to stand for 15–30 minutes, then taste, adjust seasonings and serve at room temperature.

sweet–sour mixed bean salad

This recipe has stood the test of time.

FOR 8-10 SERVINGS:
2 cups cooked green beans, in
   chunks
1–2 cups cooked kidney beans
1 small red onion, chopped
   finely
1 red or green pepper,
   chopped
¼ cup each sugar, water,
   wine vinegar and canola or
   olive oil
1 tsp salt

Put the prepared (drained) vegetables in a bowl. Add the remaining ingredients, then stir gently to mix. Cover and refrigerate for at least 24 hours before serving.

To serve, drain dressing from vegetables. (Refrigerate dressing for reuse if desired.)

tabbouleh

Bulgar (or Burghul) is made from chopped, precooked wheat grains which have a nutty flavour.

FOR 4–6 SERVINGS:
1 cup bulgar
2–3 cups boiling water
2 spring onions, chopped
¼ cup lemon juice
¼ cup olive oil
½–1 cup chopped parsley
¼–½ cup chopped mint
2 cups finely cubed tomato
salt, pepper and sugar to taste

Pour boiling water over the bulgar and leave to stand for at least 30 minutes. Drain bulgar, by pouring it into a sieve lined with a clean cloth, then gather up and twist ends of cloth to force out excess water.

Put drained bulgar in a bowl, add the next five ingredients and toss to mix. Halve tomatoes and shake out the seeds and juice. Cube flesh and add to the salad 30 minutes before serving.

Season to taste and serve at room temperature with grilled or barbecued meat or vegetables.

summer fruit salad with feta & coriander

Try this refreshing summer salad with ham, for an evening meal, or with muffins for lunch.

FOR 4–5 SERVINGS:
2 cups cubed raw nectarines
    or peaches
1 cup cubed rock melon
¼ cup crumbled feta or
    creamy blue cheese

DRESSING:
3 Tbsp freshly squeezed lime
    or lemon juice
2 Tbsp chopped coriander
pinch each of chilli powder,
    salt and sugar

Put the prepared nectarines and melon cubes in a salad bowl. Mix the dressing ingredients together and drizzle over the fruit, then sprinkle with the crumbled cheese.

gingered fruit salad

This salad is quite unlike a dessert! The fresh fruit is coated with a sharp tangy mixture of lime and fresh ginger. Fresh coriander leaves add their distinctive flavour.

FOR 4 SERVINGS:
2 cups fresh peaches, kiwifruit,
    mango or melon*
salt and caster sugar to taste
hot pepper sauce (optional)

DRESSING:
¼ cup lime juice
1–2 tsp grated fresh root ginger
1 Tbsp chopped coriander

Slice the fresh fruit into a dish. Mix the dressing ingredients together and mix them gently through the fruit. Taste and sprinkle with a little salt, caster sugar, and a few drops of hot pepper sauce if you like. Refrigerate if not serving immediately but serve at room temperature.

NOTE: If fresh coriander is hard to find, use mint instead.

*Use any fresh seasonal fruit with good flavour and texture

"taste of the tropics" salad

A salad with especially interesting flavours and contrasting textures.

FOR 2–3 SERVINGS:
1 avocado
½ papaya or rock melon
1 small red onion, finely
    chopped
about ¼ cup roasted peanuts,
    chopped coarsely

DRESSING:
2 Tbsp slivered basil leaves
2 tsp each lemon & lime juice
2 Tbsp fish sauce
1 Tbsp honey
1 Tbsp Thai chilli sauce

Measure dressing ingredients into a screw-topped jar and shake well to mix.

Seed and peel the avocado and papaya or rock melon and cube or cut in small wedges. Add the onions and peanuts. Gently toss about half the dressing through the salad, taking care not to break up the avocado and fruit. Taste and add more if you think it necessary.

Main Dish Salads

Any of these delicious salads is substantial enough to be served as a meal in its own right - just add some crusty bread for a delicious easy meal!

That said, of course they can also be served in smaller quantities as a starter course dish, or as an interesting addition to a buffet.

OPPOSITE: Pasta Niçoise, page 30

pasta niçoise (See picture on page 28)

This is based on one of our favourite salads – Salad Niçoise. We love the combination of tuna, olives and capers, and find they go really well with the pasta.

FOR 2–3 SERVINGS:
250g small pasta shells
2 eggs
150g fresh green beans
3 ripe tomatoes
12–16 black olives
1–2 Tbsp capers
1 (210g) can tuna (in oil or
   brine)
¼ cup chopped parsley

DRESSING:
½ cup mayonnaise (page 58)
2 Tbsp lemon juice
2 Tbsp olive oil
½ tsp salt
black pepper

Cook pasta in plenty of boiling water, and hard-boil 2 eggs (or add the eggs to the pasta as it cooks).

Top and tail the green beans, then boil or steam until tender. (Cook these in a sieve in the pasta water if you like.) When cooked, drain and cut into 4–5cm lengths.

In a large, shallow bowl, stir together all the dressing ingredients. Add the cubed tomatoes, cooked beans, olives and capers. Toss together gently. Open and drain the tuna, flake, but do not mash, then add this to the vegetable mixture.

Drain the cooked pasta (removing the eggs), then add the tuna mixture and the chopped parsley. Stir gently to combine. Transfer to a serving bowl (or bowls) and garnish with the quartered hard-boiled eggs.

Serve warm or at room temperature.

easy pasta salad

Ready-made pasta sauce* makes an excellent dressing with plenty of flavour for pasta salad.

FOR 4 SERVINGS:
250g spirals or other pasta

DRESSING:
1 cup bought Pasta Sauce
½ cup olive or canola oil
1 Tbsp wine vinegar
1 tsp sugar
½ tsp salt
1 tsp ground cumin
½ tsp oreganum
2–3 Tbsp lite sour cream
   (optional)

OPTIONAL INGREDIENTS:
2 spring onions, thinly sliced
2 Tbsp finely chopped parsley
1 stalk celery, thinly sliced
¼–½ cup small cubes of
   telegraph cucumber
310g can whole kernel corn
100–200g chopped ham

Cook the pasta in boiling, lightly salted water until just tender. Drain thoroughly.

Shake dressing ingredients together in a screw-topped jar. Add the sour cream for a lighter coloured, creamier dressing, if desired.

Stir about three-quarters of the dressing gently into the hot, drained pasta and refrigerate for at least 15 minutes, or up to 3 days. Just before serving, stir one or more of the optional ingredients through the pasta, and add some of the remaining dressing if you like.

*This sauce is especially useful because it does not all soak into the pasta on standing and keeps for several days in a bag in the refrigerator, ready for easy summer lunches, or barbecue accompaniments.

warm roasted vegetable and pasta salad

This combines delicious flavours and wonderful colours!

FOR 3–4 LARGE SERVINGS:
2 small red onions
6–8 cloves garlic
3 medium peppers
8 medium-large mushrooms
2 medium zucchini
½ medium eggplant
150–200g asparagus (optional)
¼ cup olive oil
2 Tbsp lemon or lime juice
250g cherry tomatoes
300g short pasta (farfalle or
   curly lasagne pieces)

DRESSING:
¼ cup olive oil
¼ cup water
2 Tbsp Balsamic vinegar
2 Tbsp lemon juice
1 Tbsp tomato paste
1 tsp Dijon or mild mustard
pepper to taste
garlic, previously roasted

Preheat the oven to 220°C. While it heats, prepare the vegetables. Peel and quarter the onions, and peel the garlic cloves. (Don't worry about the quantity of garlic – it becomes far milder as it cooks.)

Use 1 red, 1 green and 1 yellow pepper for maximum colour. Quarter or halve peppers lengthways and remove and discard seeds and pith. Remove and discard any large mushroom stems. Halve zucchini lengthways, and cut eggplant lengthways into wedges. If using asparagus, remove any tough ends.

Arrange the vegetable pieces in a single layer over the bottom of one large (or two smaller) foil or teflon-lined roasting pan(s). Combine the first measure of olive oil and lemon juice and drizzle this over the vegetables so they are all well coated.

Bake, uncovered, for 10 minutes. Turn the pieces, add the cherry tomatoes and return the mixture to the oven for a further 10 minutes. By this time, the vegetables should be beginning to brown. (If they are not, place them under the grill for a short time, until they have.)

Measure the dressing ingredients into a blender or food processor, add the cooked garlic and blend until smooth.

While vegetables roast, cook the pasta in plenty of lightly salted, boiling water. When cooked, drain and set aside.

Cut the cooked vegetables into pieces about the same size as the pasta, then gently mix with the cooked pasta and vegetables. Serve warm or cool.

NOTE: The vegetables can also be cooked on a barbecue.

'greek-style' pasta salad (See picture opposite)

This is another salad which makes a quick and delicious, one-dish summer meal.

FOR 3–4 LARGE SERVINGS:

300g short pasta shapes
(shells, spirals, crests,
penne, rigatoni, etc.)
200g feta cheese, cubed
1 large green pepper
250–300g cherry tomatoes
¼–½ cup Kalamata olives
(black or mixed)
2–3 Tbsp capers (optional)

DRESSING:

¼ cup olive oil
3 Tbsp lemon juice
1–2 Tbsp chopped fresh oreganum
1 clove garlic, minced
½ tsp salt
½ tsp sugar
black pepper to taste

Put the pasta on to cook in plenty of boiling, lightly salted water. While the pasta cooks prepare the remaining ingredients.

Measure dressing ingredients into a screw-topped jar and shake until well mixed.

Put the cubed feta in a bowl, add two tablespoons of the prepared dressing and leave to marinate for a few minutes.

Quarter and de-seed the green pepper, then cut into chunks about 1cm wide. Halve any larger tomatoes.

Drain the cooked pasta (slightly underdone is best), and rinse with plenty of cold running water. Drain well, then transfer to a large bowl. Add the feta, vegetables, olives, capers (if using) and dressing, and mix gently until well combined.

Garnish with some additional sprigs of herbs and/or capers and serve.

pasta & salsa salad

This versatile and delicious salsa can be stirred through hot pasta and served immediately or allowed to cool and served as a salad.

FOR 2-3 SERVINGS:

½–1 small red onion
1–2 cloves garlic
¼ cup lightly packed parsley,
chopped
10 fresh basil leaves, chopped
(or 1 Tbsp basil pesto)
8-12 olives, green, black or
mixed
1 Tbsp capers (optional)
6 medium tomatoes
¼ tsp sugar
salt and pepper to taste
250–300g pasta shapes (mac-
aroni, spirals etc.)
2 Tbsp olive oil

Peel and roughly chop the onion and garlic. (Adjust the quantities of these to taste, bearing in mind the sauce is not cooked.) Put the roughly chopped onion and garlic in a food processor with the parsley, basil leaves (or pesto), olives and capers. Process until well chopped but not pureed.

Halve the fresh tomatoes, scoop out and discard the seeds. Coarsely chop the flesh and add it to the food processor. Process again until the tomatoes are well chopped and everything is combined. Add the sugar and season with salt and pepper to taste.

Cook the pasta in plenty of lightly salted boiling water, then drain it and toss with the olive oil (use extra-virgin for the flavour, if you have it).

Stir the salsa through the pasta. Serve immediately, garnished with a few extra chopped olives and some fresh parsley sprigs, or refrigerate for up to 24 hours and serve cool when required.

californian pasta salad (See picture, page 4)

This is our version of the most popular salad served at Macy's food hall in San Francisco.

FOR 3-4 SERVINGS:
200g large (about 2cm) pasta
   shells
1 small head broccoli
300-400g can or jar marinated
   artichoke hearts
250g cooked peeled prawns or
   surimi
2 spring onions, finely sliced

DRESSING:
½ cup unsweetened low-fat
   yoghurt
½ cup lite sour cream
2 Tbsp lemon or lime juice
2 Tbsp chopped fresh dill
½-1 tsp salt
black pepper to taste

Cook the pasta in plenty of boiling water. Cut the broccoli into bite-sized florets and cook in a little water (or over the pasta) until just tender, then rinse with plenty of cold water.

Measure dressing ingredients into a small bowl and mix together, adding salt and pepper to taste.

Open and drain the artichoke hearts, and cut them into halves or quarters.

Drain cooked pasta (slightly underdone is best) and rinse with cold water to cool it quickly.

Combine the pasta, broccoli, and half the artichoke pieces and prawns in a large bowl. Add the dressing and the chopped spring onions, then stir gently until well combined. Arrange remaining artichoke hearts and prawns on top.

Serve alone or with crusty bread, or as part of a buffet.

soba noodle salad

Originating in Japan, these buckwheat noodles have a slightly nutty flavour.

FOR 2-3 SERVINGS:
250g soba noodles
½ small cucumber, de-seeded
1 medium carrot
¼ small daikon* (optional)
2 tsp sesame oil
1-2 Tbsp toasted sesame
   seeds

DRESSING:
2 Tbsp lime or lemon juice
2 Tbsp Kikkoman soy sauce
3-4 Tbsp canola oil
1-2 tsp finely grated fresh
   ginger

*large, mild white radish

Put the noodles on to cook in plenty of boiling water. While the noodles cook, prepare the vegetables.

Cut the cucumber, carrot and daikon into long, thin (5mm square) matchsticks. Soften the carrot sticks by plunging them briefly into boiling water.

Combine the dressing ingredients.

Drain the cooked noodles, then rinse them with plenty of cold water. Toss the cooked noodles in the sesame oil.

Tip the noodles and vegetables into a large bowl. Add the dressing and half the sesame seeds and toss together. Sprinkle with the remaining sesame seeds and serve.

ham & pasta salad with lemon-mustard dressing

Zippy lemon-mustard dressing gives the long-time salad favourites, ham and pasta, a real lift! Try this delicious salad for an easy summer meal or as part of a barbecue buffet.

FOR 4 LARGE SERVINGS:

250g large pasta shapes (route/wagon wheels, shells etc)
150–200g sliced ham
1 cup (3 medium stalks) sliced celery
2 firm ripe tomatoes
½–1 small red onion, diced
1–2 Tbsp chopped fresh chives or parsley to garnish

DRESSING:

½ cup mayonnaise (page 58)
finely grated rind of 1 lemon
¼ cup lemon juice
2 Tbsp olive or canola oil
1 Tbsp wholegrain (or Dijon) mustard
½ tsp salt
black pepper to taste

Cook the pasta in plenty of lightly salted boiling water. As soon as it is cooked, drain then cool the pasta by rinsing it in plenty of cold water. (Overcooking the pasta will result in a soggy, unpleasant salad.)

While the pasta cooks, prepare the ham and vegetables. Cut the ham into ribbons or matchsticks, slice the celery and halve, quarter, then slice the tomatoes. Dice the red onion finely, adjusting the quantity to taste.

Prepare the dressing by whisking the first six dressing ingredients together in a large bowl, then add black pepper to taste.

Add the cooled drained pasta, ham and vegetables to the dressing and stir gently to combine. Garnish with the chopped herbs and serve immediately, or store in the fridge until required (salad can be prepared several hours in advance if desired).

VARIATION: Try using ¼ cup each of lite sour cream and low fat natural (unsweetened) yoghurt in place of the mayonnaise.

peanutty noodle salad (See picture opposite)

We love salads like this, and find that a large bowlful makes an enjoyable meal. You can make it even more substantial by adding a little cold cooked or smoked chicken if you like.

FOR 4-5 SERVINGS:
250g fine egg noodles
1 large carrot
½ cup small whole green
  beans
½ small cucumber
1-2 spring onions
2 Tbsp lime or lemon juice

DRESSING:
3 Tbsp peanut butter
2 tsp sesame oil
1 Tbsp rice vinegar
1 Tbsp brown sugar
2 Tbsp Kikkoman soy sauce
1 clove garlic, minced
2 Tbsp grated fresh ginger
¼ cup hot water
2-3 Tbsp chopped coriander
1 small fresh chilli, minced
  (or ½-1 tsp chilli powder)
salt to taste (½-1 tsp)

Put all the dressing ingredients except the salt, in a screw-topped jar and shake until well mixed. Taste, and add the salt if required. Leave the dressing to stand while you prepare the remaining ingredients.

Bring a large pot of water to the boil, then add the noodles. Cook the noodles until they are just done (over-done noodles will be soggy and weak), then drain and toss with a little vegetable oil. Set aside to cool.

Cut carrot into fine strips or matchsticks, then combine with the beans in a shallow pan and boil for about 1 minute. Drain and set aside with the noodles.

Halve the cucumber lengthwise and scoop out and discard the seeds, then cut the cucumber as you did the carrot.

Cut the white section of the spring onion(s) lengthwise into fine strips (keeping some of the green part for a garnish), and add these to the other vegetables.

Toss the noodles, vegetables and dressing together in a large bowl. If possible leave to stand for 15-30 minutes, then sprinkle with the lime or lemon juice and toss again. Garnish with some chopped spring onion greens and serve.

VARIATION: Add 100-200g cold poached or smoked chicken breast, cut in fine strips.

greek salad

With crusty bread, this makes a good summer lunch. We have listed what we think are the vital ingredients.

cubed feta cheese
black olives
cubed (unpeeled) telegraph
  cucumber
tomato wedges
mild red onion rings

DRESSING FOR 4 SERVINGS:
¼ cup olive oil
1 Tbsp lemon juice
½ tsp dried oreganum
1 clove garlic, finely chopped
¼ tsp salt
pepper to taste

Prepare the salad ingredients listed using quantities to suit yourself. Place in a salad bowl. Just before serving, toss with enough dressing to coat pieces.

To make the dressing: Put all ingredients into a screw-topped jar. Shake well before use.

tomato and bread salad

This may seem an odd combination, but it is really good! Try it alone for a light weekend lunch, or serve with one-dish mains or barbecues. It's best with really flavourful red tomatoes.

FOR 4 LARGE SERVINGS:
20cm length French bread
about ¼ cup olive oil
2 tsp basil (or other) pesto
  (optional)
4 ripe red tomatoes
¼ red onion or 2 spring
  onions
about 20 basil leaves, if
  available
sprinkling of salt, sugar and
  black pepper

Cut the French bread in quarters lengthways. Mix the olive oil with the pesto if using it, then brush about half of this mixture over the bread.

Ten minutes before serving, toast bread under a moderate grill or on a barbecue, turning so that all the edges are golden but no surfaces darken.

Chop the tomatoes into 1cm cubes and put in a large salad bowl with the finely chopped onion and the basil leaves, whole or broken up by hand.

Just before serving, cut the warm, toasted bread into 15mm lengths. Sprinkle tomatoes with a little salt, sugar and pepper, toss gently, and when the juices start to run, add the bread cubes and toss to mix. Drizzle with the unused oil and serve immediately.

potato salads

American Potato Salad

An ever-popular, mildly flavoured salad! Moisten cooked waxy or new potatoes with equal amounts of wine vinegar and olive or canola oil before they cool.

Slice or cube the cooled potatoes into a bowl. For each 2 cups of potato, add a chopped spring onion, 2 tablespoons chopped parsley, ¼ cup mayonnaise (thinned to pouring consistency with a little lemon juice or milk), 1 teaspoon wine vinegar and ½ of a chopped hardboiled egg. Mix gently, without breaking up the potato too much.

Serve at room temperature topped with remaining egg, more parsley and chives.

Cumin Potato Salad

For an interesting dressing which adds zest to a potato salad, shake together in a screw-topped jar ½ cup olive or canola oil, ¼ cup wine vinegar, 2 teaspoons ground cumin, 1 tablespoon of pulp scraped from the surface of a cut onion with a teaspoon, ¾ teaspoon salt, 2 teaspoons crumbled oreganum leaves, a very finely chopped garlic clove, black pepper and hot pepper sauce to taste.

Toss cubed potato and cooked peas or chopped green beans in enough dressing to coat potato. Sprinkle with finely chopped parsley, coriander, spring onions or chives.

Spicy Yoghurt Potato Salad

Stir this low calorie dressing through cold, cubed, cooked potatoes, for a strongly flavoured salad which goes well with curries.

Finely chop together in a food processor, 1 large clove garlic, ½–1 small green chilli, ¼ cup fresh coriander, 2 spring onions, 1 teaspoon ground cumin and ½ teaspoon each sugar and salt. When finely chopped, stir in 1 cup plain unsweetened yoghurt. Gently stir dressing through cooked potatoes and serve at room temperature.

Hot Potato Salad

Cook 2–3 rashers bacon until crisp then remove from pan. Cook a finely chopped onion in 1 teaspoon bacon drippings and 1 teaspoon oil until lightly browned. Stir in 2 teaspoons flour, 1 teaspoon sugar, 2 teaspoons mixed mustard, and ¼ cup wine vinegar. Stir over low heat until dressing boils. Adjust seasoning and thin with water to pouring consistency if necessary. Slice 4 cooked new potatoes and 2 gherkins into dressing and heat through gently. Sprinkle with chopped parsley and the chopped cooked bacon before serving with frankfurters, sausages or cold meat.

gado gado salad (vegetables with peanut sauce) (See picture opposite)

Just what it is that makes this simple but substantial salad so delicious is hard to define – but it is always popular! Assemble a platter of vegetables, top with the sauce and wait for the compliments.

FOR ABOUT 1½ CUPS PEANUT SAUCE:

½ tsp tamarind paste (or 1–2 Tbsp lemon juice)
1 cup boiling water
100g roasted peanuts
1 clove garlic
1–2 tsp grated ginger
1 tsp minced chilli (or 1 small red chilli)
1 Tbsp each brown sugar and dark soy sauce

VEGETABLE PLATTER:

lettuce leaves or spinach
a selection of 3 (or more) of:
- cooked waxy or new potatoes, cubed or sliced
- green beans (or snake beans), lightly cooked
- cucumber, halved lengthways, de-seeded and sliced thinly
- sliced cabbage (or Chinese cabbage)
- tofu, cubed or sliced
- beansprouts
- hard-boiled eggs, quartered or sliced
- chopped fresh basil or coriander (optional)

To make the sauce: measure the tamarind paste into a small bowl, then add the boiling water. Break up the tamarind and leave to stand for 2–3 minutes.

Place the remaining sauce ingredients into a food processor or blender. Process briefly, then strain in the tamarind water (or lemon juice and water) and discard the tamarind pulp.

Process again to make fairly smooth paste. Transfer the sauce to a microwave bowl or pot and heat to boiling for 2–3 minutes, or until the sauce has thickened to desired consistency (about the consistency of gravy).

Set aside to cool (a little) while preparing the vegetables.

To assemble the salad: cover a platter (or individual plates) with a layer of lettuce or spinach leaves. Arrange the cubed or sliced potatoes, then any of the other suggested foods you have selected, in piles over the lettuce, finishing with a sprinkling of the chopped fresh basil or coriander if you like.

Either cover the salad generously with the peanut sauce, or serve the salad accompanied with a bowl(s) of peanut sauce so diners can help themselves.

OPTIONS: This salad is traditionally served garnished with (delicious) prawn crackers – unfortunately these have to be fried to make them puff. If you don't mind the extra oil you can add some of these (cooked in cholesterol free canola oil of course!).

Tofu may now be bought in fried cubes or cakes, as well as the 'raw' form. The cooked variety has more colour and texture so, again if you don't mind the extra calories, you may like to try using this too.

persian couscous

Colourful and tasty, with interesting textures, this makes a great side dish or even a light main, especially if you have a particularly generous hand with the fruit and nuts!

FOR 2-4 SERVINGS:

1 cup couscous
1 tsp salt
½ tsp sugar
¼–½ cup dried apricots, finely chopped
grated rind of ½ an orange (optional)
2 cups boiling water
¼–½ cup chopped almonds or pinenuts
¼–½ cup currants
2 Tbsp butter or olive oil
2 spring onions
¼ cup chopped coriander, if available

Stir the first five ingredients together in a bowl. Add the boiling water, cover and stand in a warm place for 6 minutes.

Heat the nuts and currants in the butter or oil in a small frypan, over moderate heat, until the nuts brown lightly and the currants puff up.

Stir the hot nuts and currants through the couscous. Serve hot, warm or at room temperature, adding the finely chopped spring onions and coriander just before serving.

VARIATIONS: For a more substantial salad, lightly season 200–300g lamb fillets with a little salt, pepper and ground cumin and coriander. Pan grill in a little olive oil until browned on the outside but still pink in the middle. Leave to stand for 5 minutes then cut into slices 5mm thick. Either toss through the salad or pile on top, OR stir cooked chicken (page 54) through salad when serving.

couscous & chickpea salad with orange-balsamic dressing

The orange dressing and currants give this salad an interesting, slightly sweet flavour. Add cubed, cooked chicken for a more substantial salad.

FOR 2–3 LARGE SERVINGS:

1 cup couscous
¼ cup currants
½ tsp salt
1¼ cups boiling water
300g can chickpeas
1 red pepper
2 spring onions
½ cup Kalamata olives
2–3 Tbsp chopped fresh mint

DRESSING

¼ cup orange juice
2 Tbsp Balsamic vinegar
2 Tbsp extra virgin olive oil
2 tsp ground cumin
½ tsp salt
1 clove garlic, peeled and finely chopped

Measure the couscous, currants and salt into a large bowl. Add the boiling water, then cover and leave to stand for about 5 minutes.

Open and rinse, then drain the chickpeas. Cut the pepper into cubes about the same size as the chickpeas. Thinly slice the spring onions.

Fluff the soaked couscous with a fork, then add the chickpeas, diced pepper, spring onions, olives (don't forget to warn diners if using unpitted olives) and most of the chopped mint to the bowl.

Prepare the dressing by combining all the ingredients into a screw-top jar, then shaking to combine.

Pour in the dressing and toss salad to combine, then garnish with the remaining chopped mint.

brown rice salad

This salad has a lovely flavour. Served cold or warm it makes an excellent addition to a buffet and makes an interesting vegetarian meal. Follow the instructions precisely for best results.

FOR 6 SERVINGS:
1 cup uncooked brown rice
1¾ cups water
¼ cup Kikkoman soy sauce
½ medium onion, finely chopped
1 red pepper, chopped into tiny cubes
3 spring onions, finely chopped
½ cup sultanas
½ cup roasted peanuts, coarsely chopped
½ cup each roasted sunflower, pumpkin, and sesame seeds (page 60)

DRESSING:
¼ cup olive or canola oil
2 Tbsp lemon juice
1 tsp grated lemon rind
1 clove garlic, crushed
1 tsp grated fresh root ginger
1 tsp honey or sugar

Place rice and unsalted water in a tightly covered pot and simmer for 45 minutes, or until the rice is tender and the water has all been absorbed.

Add the soy sauce and finely chopped onion to the hot, cooked rice, mix well, then leave for at least 2 hours or overnight if you have the time.

Measure all dressing ingredients into a screw-topped jar or food processor and process or shake well to mix.

Shortly before serving, add remaining salad ingredients and dressing, and mix well. Leftover salad may be refrigerated and used over the next few days, with relatively little loss of quality.

peanutty rice salad

This salad makes a great lunch if you have cooked rice on hand.

FOR 2 SERVINGS:
2 cups cooked rice
½ cup cooked peas
½ cup chopped roasted peanuts
1 grated carrot
2 spring onions

DRESSING:
2 tsp sesame oil
2 Tbsp olive or canola oil
1 Tbsp light soy sauce

Measure everything, including the dressing ingredients, into a large plastic bag or serving bowl. Toss everything together lightly. Taste, and add more sesame oil if you want a stronger flavour, and chill until salad is needed.

sushi rice salad (See picture opposite)

This salad is sure to become a talking point of any meal – it contains all the delicious ingredients of conventional sushi, but is even easier to prepare because, instead of being neatly rolled up, everything is just tossed together!

FOR 2–3 SERVINGS:
1 cup medium-grain rice
2 cups boiling water
50–100g cold-smoked salmon
   (or 100-200g surimi)
pickled pink ginger (optional)
2–3 sheets yaki nori (grilled
   seaweed sheets)
1 avocado, peeled and cubed
½ a telegraph cucumber,
   cubed
1 medium carrot, finely diced

DRESSING:
2 Tbsp sherry
2 Tbsp canola oil
1 Tbsp Kikkoman soy sauce
1 Tbsp wine or rice vinegar
1 Tbsp sugar
½ tsp salt
1–2 tsp wasabi paste
1–2 tsp grated fresh ginger
   (optional)

The rice and dressing may be prepared in advance, but the salad itself is best assembled shortly before serving.

Add boiling water to rice, then cover and microwave at 50% power for 15 minutes or until the grains are completely tender. While the rice cooks, measure all the dressing ingredients into a screw-topped jar, then shake until blended.

When the rice is cooked, pour in half the dressing and stir until well combined. Leave the rice to stand until cool. (Refrigerate if preparing in advance.)

Cut the salmon into strips about 1cm wide (or shred the surimi) and slice the ginger into thin strips. Cut or tear the nori sheets into strips about 1cm wide and 4cm long.

Cube the vegetables, then stir into the rice along with most of the salmon (or surimi), ginger and nori (reserving a little for garnishing) and the remaining dressing. Toss to combine.

Garnish with the reserved salmon and nori strips and serve. Accompany with little bowls of extra soy sauce and wasabi if desired.

confetti rice salad

This nutritious salad may be served hot, warm or cold.

FOR 4 SERVINGS:
1 large onion, chopped
2 cloves garlic, chopped
¼ cup canola or olive oil
1 cup basmati rice
½ cup red lentils
3 Tbsp wine vinegar
1 tsp salt
2 tsp sugar
2 tsp Dijon or mild mustard
3 cups boiling water

Chop onion into small pieces. Heat chopped onion, garlic and oil in a large covered microwave dish on High (100%) power for 2 minutes. Stir in the rice, lentils, vinegar, salt, sugar and mustard and boiling water. Cover and cook on Medium (50%) power for 20 minutes, then stand for 10 minutes or longer before adding some of the following: chopped parsley, spring onions, red or green peppers, celery or radishes, cooked green peas or corn kernels, grated carrots. Serve plain or tossed with sesame dressing (page 60).

10 minute salmon and couscous salad

Try this quick recipe for an easy dinner at the end of a long, hot summer day.

FOR 2-3 SERVINGS:

1 can (100–200g) salmon
1½ cups liquid (see method)
½ tsp minced chilli (optional)
¾ cup couscous
2 spring onions, chopped
2 cups chopped crisp lettuce
  leaves
about 1 cup chopped
  cucumber
1–2 stalks celery, chopped
fresh coriander, basil, dill
about 1 cup coarsely chopped
  tomatoes
juice of 1 lemon
2–3 Tbsp olive oil
salt and pepper to taste

Use whatever sized can of salmon you have handy. Drain liquid from salmon can into a measuring jug and make up to 1½ cups with chicken or other stock. Add the chilli if using it, then bring to the boil in a pot or microwave oven.

Sprinkle in the couscous, remove from heat, cover container and leave to stand for 6 minutes, while you prepare everything else.

Chop all the vegetables except the tomatoes into a shallow salad bowl. (Add other vegetables or make replacements if desired). Add whatever herbs you have and like. (Cover and refrigerate if not using immediately).

Just before serving, toss the salmon through the room-temperature couscous with half the lemon juice and oil. Taste this mixture and season carefully if necessary, then fork it gently through the vegetables, toss gently with the remaining lemon juice and oil, top with the tomatoes and serve straight away.

VARIATIONS: Add some cooked prawns or chopped marinated mussels, surimi, or chopped hardboiled eggs, when combining the vegetables and couscous mixture.

fisherman's salad with kiwi salsa

Use fresh or saltwater fish for this salad.

FOR 4 SERVINGS:

1 cleaned whole 1kg fish,
  skin on
1 tsp each celery, garlic and
  onion salt
1 tsp hickory smoke salt
1 tsp lemon pepper
1 tsp ground cumin
1 tsp oreganum
2 lemons
fresh herb sprigs if available
about 1 Tbsp canola oil

Cut several deep slashes on each side of cleaned fish. Place on a double layer of foil. Sprinkle the dry seasonings in and over the fish. Squeeze juice from 1 lemon in and over the fish. Slice other lemon and place in the cavity, with fresh herbs if available. Drizzle oil over the fish. Seal fish in foil so you can turn parcel. Place in a large shallow baking dish.

Bake a 1kg fish (5cm thick, side to side) at 180°C for about 20 minutes, until flesh at thickest part is milky white and will flake. Cool for 10 minutes. Pour off, strain and save all juice. Discard head, tail, fins and skin, then lift flesh from bones in chunks. Put in a dish with the juice (warm gently if juice sets). Taste, add extra salt if needed.

Serve at room temperature with Kiwi Salsa tossed through fish and mayonnaise alongside.

kiwi salsa

2 cups chopped kiwifruit
3 spring onions, sliced
½ cup basil leaves, chopped
¼—½ tsp finely chopped red
    or green chilli
1 tsp ground cumin
¼ cup lemon juice
salt and pepper to taste

Gently stir all ingredients together so the kiwifruit keeps its shape. Refrigerate for up to 24 hours in a covered container, or fold through the cold flaked fish as desired.

VARIATION: Replace the kiwifruit with any other fresh, raw fruit.

seared scallop salad

Scallops are at their best when cooked briefly in a very hot pan. Served with this dressing, they make a memorable salad.

FOR 4 SERVINGS:
about 6 cups mixed salad
    greens
1 avocado
about 1 Tbsp lime or lemon
    juice
about 10cm cucumber
½ cup chopped coriander
about 20 cherry tomatoes
about 500g scallops
1 tsp sesame oil
1 tsp soy sauce
freshly ground black pepper
oil for cooking

DRESSING:
¼—½ tsp minced chilli
1 clove garlic, finely chopped
2 tsp finely grated ginger
    (optional)
1 Tbsp sugar
1 Tbsp wine vinegar or rice
    vinegar
¼ cup water
2 Tbsp fish sauce
1 Tbsp sesame oil
1 Tbsp lemon or lime juice

Make the dressing, measuring dressing ingredients into a screw-topped jar and shaking well to mix. Refrigerate up to a week.

Prepare the salad greens, putting them into a large plastic bag or covered bowl to chill. Just before you start to cook the scallops, slice the avocado, turn slices in the lemon or lime juice, slice the cucumber into chunky pieces and chop the coriander leaves.

Prepare the scallops, patting them dry and tossing in the sesame oil and soy sauce.

Heat a film of oil in a large, non-stick pan, on a high heat until very hot. Add the scallops in batches and toss for 2–3 minutes, letting surfaces brown lightly. Take care not to overcook. Remove from pan and reheat pan before cooking more. When all scallops are cooked, add pepper to taste, then spoon a little dressing over them and leave to cool.

Just before serving, arrange the salad greens and the other salad ingredients on individual plates. Arrange the scallops on the greens and sprinkle the remaining dressing over everything.

Serve immediately, with warmed crusty bread rolls.

VARIATIONS: Cook salmon or other fresh fish in the same way. Flake after cooked fish has cooled in the dressing and use in the salad. Freshly cooked mussels also make a good salad. Steam them open, remove from their shells and leave to stand in the dressing.

east-west beef salad with coriander dressing (See picture opposite)

The strong and delicious flavours in the dressing of this salad are intended for those who like strong Asian seasonings.

FOR 2 SERVINGS:
200–250g rump steak cut 2cm thick
1 Tbsp fish or soy sauce
1 Tbsp canola oil
mixed salad leaves
cucumber chunks
cherry tomatoes
sliced cooked green beans
avocado slices
basil leaves

DRESSING:
1–2 cloves garlic, finely chopped
1 tsp finely chopped lemon grass
2 Tbsp sugar
1 Tbsp fish sauce
2 Tbsp fresh lime juice
2 Tbsp water
¼ tsp salt
⅛ tsp chilli powder or minced red chilli
2–3 Tbsp chopped coriander
1 chopped spring onion

Trim any fat from the steak. Coat steak with a little soy sauce and oil and leave to marinate for at least 15 minutes, or up to 24 hours in the refrigerator.

Prepare the salad ingredients, if necessary make two salads in shallow bowls.

About 15 minutes before serving, preheat a heavy pan over high heat and pan-grill steak in the dry pan for 1–2 minutes per side until brown on the outside but pink in the middle. Put steak on a carving board and leave to cool.

To make the **East-West Coriander Dressing**, finely chop the garlic and thinly sliced lemon grass in a food processor or blender. Add the remaining dressing ingredients and process until coriander and spring onion leaves are chopped.

Just before serving, slice the cooled meat thinly into strips and coat with part of the dressing. Arrange slices on the individual salads and drizzle over extra dressing. Serve with crusty bread or with bowls of Basmati or Jasmine rice.

NOTE: Replace rump with sirlion, rib-eye or fillet steak if desired.

sesame lamb salad

This very special lamb salad should be served as the main course of a summer meal, with warm bread rolls, or bowls of plain rice.

FOR 2 SERVINGS:
1 boneless lamb loin (about 200g)
½ tsp canola oil
1 clove garlic, finely chopped
1 Tbsp Kikkoman soy sauce
1 tsp sesame oil
2-3 cups prepared salad vegetables
fresh herbs, as desired
few sprigs watercress
2 kiwifruit

DRESSING:
1 Tbsp Kikkoman soy sauce
1 Tbsp wine vinegar
2 tsp sugar
¼–½ tsp wasabi (optional)
¼ cup canola oil
½ tsp sesame oil

Sauté the boneless loin in the canola oil in a non-stick pan over moderate heat for 6 minutes, turning several times. Remove from heat and add garlic, soy sauce and sesame oil. Turn meat and leave to cool in this marinade for 15 minutes.

Shake all the dressing ingredients together in a screw-topped jar. Prepare salad vegetables for two large salads, adding herbs and edible flowers such as **borage, pansies** and **calendula petals** if desired. Break watercress sprigs into smaller pieces, if these are available. Slice peeled kiwifruit 5mm thick.

Slice lamb thinly and turn in marinade, adding 2 tsp dressing. Toss prepared salad in half the dressing and arrange on large, individual plates.

Arrange warm lamb slices on the salad vegetables and serve immediately. (Save remaining dressing for another salad.)

mediterranean meat salad

A great way to serve meat on a hot day!

FOR 4-6 SERVINGS:
500g sliced roast (lean) beef fillet or lamb loin
1 red onion, thinly sliced

DRESSING:
¼ cup canola oil
2-3 Tbsp wine vinegar
2 Tbsp chopped parsley
2 Tbsp chopped capers
1-2 tsp Dijon mustard
½ tsp oreganum
1 tsp salt
1 tsp Worcestershire sauce

Use meat which is cooked so it is rare or pink. Arrange the sliced meat and onions on a platter, in overlapping slices. Cover and refrigerate until needed.

Mix the dressing ingredients in a small bowl or shake in a screw-topped jar, using the smaller quantities of vinegar and mustard initially, adding extra after you have tasted the dressing, if necessary. Fifteen minutes before serving, drizzle the dressing over the sliced meat and onions, cover with cling film and refrigerate until you are ready to serve.

NOTE: Onion flavour will become milder on standing.

sausage and potato salad with mustard dressing

New potatoes and sliced precooked sausages taste great when mixed with this dressing! Make the salad with your favourite (precooked) specialty deli sausages, frankfurters, or even leftover barbecued sausages.

FOR 4 SERVINGS:
about 300g new potatoes
200–300g cooked sausages
  (see above)
4 gherkins (optional)
2–4 pickled onions (optional)
crisp, coarsely chopped lettuce

DRESSING:
¼ cup grainy mustard
2 Tbsp brown sugar
2 Tbsp wine vinegar
1 large clove garlic, chopped
1 Tbsp roughly chopped
  parsley
1 Tbsp roughly chopped chives
  or spring onions
1 Tbsp chopped coriander
  (optional)
½ cup olive or canola oil
¼ cup warm water

Scrape the new potatoes and simmer in just enough lightly salted water to cover them. Cook until tender, testing with a sharp knife. Remove from heat, leave to stand in the water for 5 minutes.

Make the **Mustard Dressing** in a food processor or blender. (The recipe makes more than you need for this salad, but ingredients are given in convenient quantities.) Measure the first 3 dressing ingredients into the bowl of the machine. If the grainy mustard you use is sweet, start with half the amount of brown sugar. Add the roughly chopped garlic, parsley, chives or spring onions. The coriander adds a lovely flavour but is not essential. Add it if you can.

Add the oil slowly with the motor running, then add the water. Taste and add extra sugar if required. The finished dressing should be of a thickness somewhere between mayonnaise and French dressing. Use immediately or refrigerate in a covered container, but bring to room temperature before using.

Drain potatoes, slice and toss gently in enough dressing to coat while warm. Slice sausages for salad about 5mm thick and toss in enough dressing to coat. Leave to stand for a few minutes if possible, so the dressing will flavour the sausages.

Gently mix the prepared sausages and potatoes together and add the finely sliced or chopped gherkins and/or pickled onions if desired.

To serve, make a bed of torn or chopped lettuce on individual plates (or shallow bowls) and pile the sausage mixture on top.

chicken waldorf salad (See picture opposite)

This chicken salad with its contrasting textures, makes an interesting meal at times when summer fruits are not available.

FOR 2–3 SERVINGS:
150–200g cooked chicken*
1–1½ crisp red apples
2 Tbsp lemon juice
2 stalks celery
¼ cup shelled walnuts,
   roughly chopped
mixed salad herbs
2–3 cups salad greens

DRESSING:
1 Tbsp sugar
¾ tsp salt
1 tsp curry powder or paste
1½ tsp Dijon or mild mustard
2 Tbsp each lemon juice, lite
   sour cream and canola oil
2–3 Tbsp chicken stock or
   water

To prepare **Curried Sour Cream Mustard Dressing**, whisk together first seven dressing ingredients in a small bowl until smooth. Thin with a little water or chicken stock until coating consistency.

*Slice or dice flesh from the breast or leg of moist grilled, baked or roast chicken, bought pre-cooked chicken or smoked chicken. Using a sharp knife, slice it attractively, or cut in 1cm cubes. If not using immediately, cover tightly and refrigerate.

Wash salad greens and any fresh herbs you would like in the salad, roll up in a paper towel (as you would roll a sponge roll), then refrigerate until needed.

Assemble salad a short time before serving. Cut unpeeled apples into wedges or cubes, put in a large bowl and sprinkle with lemon juice. Cut celery into 5mm thick slices or cubes, then add to the apples, along with the cooked chicken, walnuts and salad herbs.

Add enough thinned dressing to coat, and toss together. Make a bed of torn or chopped salad greens on individual plates (or shallow bowls).

Pile mixed salad on top of greens and serve with the remaining dressing for diners to add if desired.

chicken & crispy noodle salad (See picture on page 1)

This tasty and interesting salad has a low-fat dressing, and makes a great lunch or dinner on a hot day.

FOR 2 SERVINGS:

2 boneless, skinless chicken
  breasts
1 tsp sesame oil
1 tsp Kikkoman soy sauce
2–3 cups crisp lettuce
salad vegetables:
  spring onion
  coriander leaves
  celery
  cucumber
  red pepper
  sprouts
about 1 cup crisp-fried
  noodles*
1 Tbsp toasted sesame seeds
  or 2 Tbsp chopped roasted
  peanuts

DRESSING:

2 cloves garlic
1cm piece of fresh ginger
1 small dried chilli
¼ cup wine vinegar or rice
  vinegar
¼ cup Kikkoman soy sauce
2 Tbsp sugar
1 Tbsp sesame oil
1 Tbsp cornflour
½ cup water

First, make the dressing. Chop the garlic and ginger in a food processor or blender. Add remaining dressing ingredients except water and process until very finely chopped, then add the water, process briefly, and tip into a pot or pan. Bring to the boil, then cool by standing container in cold water. Use about ¼ cup dressing for salad and refrigerate remainder.

Pound chicken breasts between two sheets of plastic until 1cm thick, then coat with sesame oil and soy sauce and grill or pan-grill until juices no longer run pink when flesh is pierced. Put aside to cool.

Cut the crisp lettuce into strips about 1cm wide and 6-8 cm long. Place in a bowl with two or three other salad vegetables, cut into easily managed pieces.

To assemble, slice warm chicken breasts into diagonal strips 1cm thick. Toss these with about 1 tablespoon of the cooled dressing.

Toss the salad mixture gently with about 2 tablespoons of dressing.

Layer the greens, crisp-fried noodles and chicken in a pyramid on two salad plates and serve immediately, drizzled with a little extra dressing if desired.

Sprinkle with sesame seeds or peanuts.

*Crisp-fried (or crispy) noodles can now be bought pre-packaged or from the bulk foods department of most large supermarkets.

chicken and kumara salad with curried sour cream-mango dressing

Chicken coated with curry-flavoured mayonnaise has long been an American favourite, but we find that creamy dressings based on sour cream are easier to make and are even nicer.

FOR 2-3 SERVINGS:
150–200g cooked chicken*
400g golden fleshed kumara
2–3 cups salad greens
mixed salad herbs (optional)
¼ cup chopped roast peanuts
  or cashews

DRESSING:
¼ cup lite sour cream
1–1½ tsp curry powder or
  paste
2 Tbsp mango chutney,
  chopped
½ tsp salt
2–3 Tbsp chicken stock or
  water

To prepare **Curried Sour Cream–Mango Dressing**, stir together the first four dressing ingredients in a small bowl until smooth. Thin with a little water or chicken stock until dressing is coating consistency and then put aside.

*Slice or dice flesh from the breast or leg of moist grilled, baked or roast chicken, bought pre-cooked chicken or smoked chicken. Using a sharp knife, slice it attractively, or cut in 1cm cubes. If not using immediately, cover tightly and refrigerate.

Scrub and cut the ends off the kumara, then wrap in cling-film and microwave until flesh 'gives' when pressed, probably between 5 and 6 minutes. Leave to cool.

Wash salad greens and any fresh herbs you would like in the salad, break into suitable pieces, roll up in a paper towel (as you would roll a sponge roll) then refrigerate until needed.

To assemble salad, peel off kumara skin and slice. Toss the cooked kumara together with the cooked chicken, most of the nuts, the salad herbs and greens, and the thinned dressing. Arrange salad on individual plates, and sprinkle with remaining nuts. Serve with the extra dressing for diners to add as desired.

Reference Recipes

These recipes are simply a collection of...well, everything!

Some are referred to throughout the book, while others are just personal favourites or important ideas that defied categorisation and were simply too good to be left out.

Whatever the reason for their inclusion, we're sure you'll find them useful!

OPPOSITE: Pesto, page 58

pesto (See picture on page 56)

Fresh basil has a wonderful flavour but a short season. Making pesto is a way of enjoying it all year.

FOR ABOUT 1 CUP:

1½–2 cups tightly packed basil leaves
½ cup parsley
2 cloves garlic
2–4 Tbsp parmesan cheese
2 Tbsp pinenuts, almonds or walnuts
¼–½ cup olive oil
about ½ tsp salt

Wash the basil to minimise later browning, then drain on a cloth or paper towel. Remove tough stems and put basil, parsley and peeled garlic cloves in a food processor with the parmesan cheese and nuts. Process, adding up to ¼ cup of oil, until finely chopped. Keep adding oil until you have a dark green paste, just liquid enough to pour. Add salt to taste.

Pour into a sterilised jar and top with extra oil to prevent browning. Refrigerate up to three months, or freeze for longer storage.

pesto dressing

Pesto dressing is delicious used on leafy green or rice and pasta salads, and also makes an excellent marinade for cooked vegetables.

Add 1–2 tablespoons of pesto to French dressing (page 11), use within 24 hours; OR shake ¼ cup olive oil together with 1–2 tablespoons of pesto and 1 teaspoon wine vinegar or lemon juice and use immediately.

mayonnaise

Quick and easy to make in the food processor, this sauce is delicious and versatile. It puts most bought mayonnaise to shame!

FOR ABOUT 1½ CUPS:

1 egg
½ tsp each salt and sugar
1 tsp Dijon or mild mustard
2 Tbsp wine vinegar
about 1 cup olive or canola oil

Measure everything except the oil into a food processor or blender. Turn on and add the oil in a thin stream until the mayonnaise is as thick and creamy as you like it. Keep in a covered container in the refrigerator for up to three weeks.

tofu "mayonnaise"

Based on tofu, this dressing contains no eggs and little oil - it makes a good 'lite' alternative to conventional mayonnaise.

FOR ABOUT 1 CUP:
1–2 cloves garlic
3 Tbsp chopped fresh herbs (basil, parsley and/or chives)
1 cup (250-300g) crumbled tofu
¼ cup olive or canola oil
1 Tbsp white wine vinegar
juice of ½ lemon
1 tsp Dijon or mild mustard
½ tsp each salt and sugar

Chop garlic and herbs in a food processor or blender – don't be too generous with the garlic or the dressing will taste of little else. Add the remaining ingredients and process until smooth.

Store refrigerated in an air-tight container for 1–2 weeks.

tex-mex dressing

Use this assertive dressing to liven up gently flavoured foods — spoon it into avocado halves and stir it into canned drained beans to make spicy bean salads.

FOR ¾ CUP DRESSING:
½ cup olive oil
1 tsp ground cumin
1 tsp salt
1 tsp sugar
½ tsp dried oreganum
½ tsp paprika
¼–½ tsp chilli paste
1–2 cloves garlic, very finely chopped
2 tsp prepared smooth mustard
1 Tbsp tomato paste
1 Tbsp wine vinegar
2 Tbsp boiling water

Measure the first seven ingredients into a screw-topped jar and shake well to mix.

Mix the very finely chopped garlic, mustard, tomato paste and wine vinegar in a cup or small bowl. Stir in the boiling water to make a smooth paste, then transfer to the jar holding the other ingredients and stir well, then shake thoroughly until smooth and thick.

Leave to stand for at least 30 minutes before using. Refrigerate up to a week.

toasted seeds & nuts

Combine ½ cup each sunflower seeds, pumpkin seeds and chopped raw (skin on) almonds. Toss them in ½ teaspoon of sesame oil and cook in a heavy pan over a low heat, shaking the pan at intervals, for 5–10 minutes. When pumpkin seeds look plump, remove from heat and cool. Store in a screw-topped jar. Sprinkle a few tablespoons into colesaw (or other salads) when serving.

croutons

Croutons make a wonderful addition to many salads.

In a frypan over low heat, warm 2 tablespoons olive oil with 1 clove sliced garlic without browning. Cut two slices white bread (toast thickness) into small cubes and toss in the garlic oil, then cook on medium heat, turning frequently, until croutons are golden brown, about 20 minutes.

If preferred, brown under a grill, checking regularly to prevent uneven browning. Or bake at 150°C for about 5 minutes or until golden brown.

sesame dressing

This strongly flavoured dressing is addictive! It turns the simplest coleslaw vegetables into something exciting, but also dresses tomato, sprout, mesclun, cooked vegetable and pasta salads successfully, too. It keeps well and may be refrigerated for weeks.

FOR ¾ CUP DRESSING:
¼ cup canola oil
2 Tbsp sesame oil
2 Tbsp wine vinegar
1 Tbsp lemon or lime juice
2 Tbsp sugar
1 Tbsp Thai sweet chilli sauce
1 Tbsp Dijon or mild mustard
1 tsp salt
1 tsp Balsamic vinegar if
   available

Measure all ingredients into a screw-topped jar and shake together. Use about 2 teaspoons dressing to 1 cup of compact salad, or 1 teaspoon per cup of salad leaves.

For a milder dressing use only 1 tablespoon sesame oil.

roasted vegetable salad dressing

If you like a dressing with a definite flavour on roasted vegetables, try this!

2 Tbsp lemon juice (or 1 Tbsp
  wine vinegar)
1 tsp sugar
2–3 Tbsp olive or canola oil
¼ teaspoon salt
one or more of:
  2 anchovy fillets, finely
  chopped
  2 tsp chopped capers
  2 tsp Dijon mustard
  2 tsp basil pesto

Mix everything together in a food processor or shake together in a screw-topped jar. Store in an airtight container.

poppy seed dressing

Honey and orange juice give this dressing a pleasant sweetness, Balsamic vinegar an interesting tang, and the poppy seeds add crunchy texture as well as an unusual appearance.

¼ cup canola oil
2 Tbsp honey
3 Tbsp lemon juice
1 Tbsp Balsamic vinegar
finely grated rind of ½ orange
¼ tsp salt
2 Tbsp poppy seeds

Use on grated carrot, roasted vegetables, fruit and avocado salads, as well as coleslaw – we like it on almost any salad.

Measure the first six ingredients into a blender or food processor. Blend thoroughly then add the poppy seeds. Blend very briefly then transfer to a screw-topped jar for storage.

seasoned oil

Use this flavoured oil for brushing vegetables before roasting, or when making croutons. Try it in dressings too, for extra flavour.

½ cup olive or canola oil
2 peeled cloves garlic
6 roughly chopped basil
  leaves,
1–2 Tbsp fresh thyme
1–2 Tbsp fresh rosemary

Measure all ingredients into a food processor fitted with its metal chopping blade. Process until finely chopped. Stand in a sunny place or heat to bath temperature. Leave for at least 10 minutes then strain, discarding flavourings. Store leftover oil in an airtight jar or bottle in a cool place.

Index

Knives by Mail Order

For about 20 years I have imported my favourite, very sharp, kitchen knives from Switzerland. They keep their edges well, are easy to sharpen, a pleasure to use, and make excellent gifts.

VEGETABLE KNIFE $8.00
Ideal for cutting and peeling vegetables, these knives have a straight edged 85mm blade and black (dishwasher-proof) nylon handle. Each knife comes in an individual plastic sheath.

BONING/UTILITY KNIFE $9.50
Excellent for boning chicken and other meats, and/or general kitchen duties. Featuring a 103mm blade that curves to a point and a dishwasher-proof, black nylon handle, each knife comes in a plastic sheath.

SERRATED KNIFE $9.50
I find these knives unbelievably useful and I'm sure you will too! They are perfect for cutting cooked meats, ripe fruit and vegetables, and slicing bread and baking. Treated carefully, these blades stay sharp for years. The serrated 110mm blade is rounded at the end with a black (dishwasher-proof) nylon handle. Each knife comes in an individual plastic sheath.

THREE-PIECE SET $20.00
This three-piece set includes a vegetable knife, a serrated knife (as described above) and a right-handed potato peeler with a matching black handle, presented in a white plastic wallet.

GIFT BOXED KNIFE SET $44.00
This set contains five knives plus a matching right-handed potato peeler. There is a straight bladed vegetable knife and a serrated knife (as above), as well as a handy 85mm serrated blade vegetable knife, a small (85mm) utility knife with a pointed tip and a smaller (85mm) serrated knife. These elegantly presented sets make ideal gifts.

SERRATED CARVING KNIFE $28.50
This fabulous knife cuts beautifully and is a pleasure to use. The 21cm serrated blade does not require sharpening. Once again the knife has a black moulded, dishwasher safe handle and comes in a plastic sheath.

STEEL $20.00
The steel has a 20cm blade and measures 33cm in total. With its matching black handle the steel is an ideal companion to your own knives, or as a gift. I have had excellent results using the steel. N.B. Not for use with serrated knives.

PROBUS SPREADER/SCRAPER $5.50
After my knives, this is the most used tool in my kitchen! With a comfortable plastic handle, metal shank and flexible plastic blade (suitable for use on non-stick surfaces), these are excellent for mixing muffin batters, stirring and scraping bowls, spreading icings, turning pikelets etc., etc....

NON-STICK TEFLON LINERS
I regard these Teflon liners as another essential kitchen item – they really help avoid the frustration of stuck-on baking, roasting or frying. Once you've used them, you'll wonder how you did without!

Round tin liner (for 15-23cm tins)	$5.50
Round tin liner (for 23-30cm tins)	$8.50
Square tin liner (for 15-23cm tins)	$5.50
Square tin liner (for 23-30cm tins)	$8.50
Ring tin liner (for 23cm tins)	$5.95
Baking sheet liner (33x44cm)	$10.95

Prices as at 1 October 1999, all prices include GST. Please add $3.50 post & packing to any knife/spreader order (any number of items). Please note, Teflon prices **include** post & packing.

Make cheques payable to Alison Holst Mail Orders and post to:

Alison Holst Mail Orders
Freepost 124807
PO Box 17016
Wellington